PREGNANCY

Kirsten Lamb

RAINTREE
STECK-VAUGHN
RSVP PUBLISHERS

A Harcourt Company

Austin   New York
www.raintreesteckvaughn.com

Library of Congress Cataloging-in-Publication Data

Lamb, Kirsten.
    Pregnancy / Kirsten Lamb.
        p. cm. -- (Health issues)
    Includes bibliographical references and index.
    ISBN 0-7398-4418-0
    1. Pregnancy--Juvenile literature. 2. Childbirth--Juvenile literature. [1. Pregnancy.] I.
Title. II. Series.

RG556 .L345 2001
618.2'4--dc21
                                                                00-054292

Printed in Italy. Bound in the United States.

1 2 3 4 5 6 7 8 9 0 LB 05 04 03 02 01

Acknowledgments

The author and publishers thank the following for their permission to reproduce photographs and illustrations: Corbis Images: pages 23 (Laura Dwight), 37 (April Saul), 38 (right), 42 (Arvind Garg), 43 (Bettmann), 49 (Pablo Corral V), 58 (left) (Owen Franken), 58 (right) (Liba Taylor); Angela Hampton Family Life Pictures: cover and pages 1, 5, 16, 19, 20, 22, 24, 32, 33, 35, 41, 46; Impact Photo (Robin Laurance): page 38 (left); Panos Pictures: page 57 (Giacomo Pirozzi); Photofusion: pages 4 (Paul Baldesare), 11 (Paul Baldesare), 34 (Tim Dub), 40 (Paul Baldesare), 59 (Liam Bailey); Popperfoto: pages 15, 26 (bottom), 53, 56; Science Photo Library: pages 6 (D. Phillips), 13 (Hattie Young), 14 (Dr G. Moscoso), 26 (top) (Jim Varney), 27 (James Stevenson), 54 (Richard Rawlins/Custom Medical Stock Photo); Wayland Picture Library: pages 7 (Michael Courtney), 9 (Zak Waters), 10 (Michael Courtney), 12 (Zul Mukhida), 21 (Michael Courtney), 45, 47 (Jeff Issac Greenberg); www.JohnBirdsall.co.uk: pages 28, 29. The illustration on page 8 was drawn by Michael Courtney. The illustrations on pages 17, 30, 50, 51, and 52 were drawn by Carole Binding.

Contents

Introduction
Why Should I Know About Pregnancy?

Pregnancy is an exciting, normal, and natural event. It is the wonderful creation of a new life and ends in the birth of a new baby.

Is knowing about pregnancy relevant to young people? The answer is yes. Many young people want to think about their future and the idea of someday having a family of their own. They want to know how to avoid an unplanned pregnancy, and to learn about the consequences of pregnancy. Knowing the facts and understanding the issues, as they may affect you, helps you to make informed choices about your future.

Your teenage years can be both exciting and confusing. This is because teenagers are just starting to develop close relationships with others and are learning how to make their own decisions about sexual relationships. These new feelings and experiences can be pretty confusing! Talking about them to your parents or friends can be difficult and embarrassing.

Thinking about your own sexuality and understanding the impact that it has on you can help you talk about your feelings and experiences with your parents, your partner, or your friends. It can help you decide when to start having sexual relationships, and how to protect yourself from unwanted pregnancy or sexually transmitted infections if you do choose to begin having sex.

Having a baby has a huge impact on a person's life. Babies and their parents all have needs that have to be fulfilled. Ask yourself what it would be like to be pregnant and become a parent while still a teenager. Would you be able to fulfill the needs of your baby and yourself?

Read on and see how a normal pregnancy starts, progresses, and ends in the delivery of a new baby. There are ways to plan for a healthy pregnancy and the delivery of a healthy baby. Even as a teenager, the way you live now may affect your future ability to have children.

Chapter 5 looks at the options for people who get pregnant when they don't want to be. Teenagers in this situation often find themselves confused about what to do and often don't know how to get help. This chapter will discuss some of the choices that are available, such as having the baby, abortion, foster care, and adoption. There are many different feelings about these choices, and it is up to the individual to decide what is the best choice for them.

Unwanted pregnancy can usually be avoided. Contraception is safe and available. Knowing about it will help you take action to protect yourself from pregnancy and sexually transmitted diseases. You have the right to choose what method is right for you.

What about the future? The final chapter looks at developments in contraception and fertility management that might come about during your lifetime, and challenges you to think about what is "right" for human life.

The facts
I'd rather know the real facts than rely on crazy stuff I hear from my friends.

1 Conception
How Pregnancy Begins

Two Halves Make a Whole, or The Genetics of Conception

Technically speaking, the very first thing that must happen to make a baby is the meeting of sperm and egg. Sperm are the male sex cells which are produced in the male body. Eggs are the female sex cells. The sperm and egg meet when a man and a woman have sexual intercourse, or when he puts his penis inside of her vagina. Both the sperm and the egg contain half of the genetic material needed to make one human cell. Each one (the sperm or the egg) contains half the genetic material needed to make one human cell. That human cell contains a nucleus, which in turn contains chromosomes—microscopic threads made up of about 2,000 genes each. Chromosomes contain all the individual

Sperm and egg

A single sperm penetrates the wall of an egg. This false-colored picture is magnified by about 800 times.

Girl or boy?

All human cells contain 46 chromosomes, consisting of 44 ordinary chromosomes and 2 sex chromosomes known as X or Y chromosomes. The first cell of a new baby is created by joining a sperm and an egg, each of which provides 22 ordinary chromosomes and one sex chromosome. The sex chromosome in a sperm may be either an X or a Y. The sex chromosome in an egg is always an X. If a sperm containing an X chromosome fertilizes an egg, the baby will be a girl. If a sperm containing a Y chromosome fertilizes an egg, the baby will be a boy.

genetic information that makes us precisely who we are. They determine, for example, our hair and eye color, and our blood type.

Sperm Production

Sperm are produced in the testes of men. The two testes sit in the sac called the scrotum, which is a bag of skin. The temperature inside the scrotum is less than that in the body, and this cooler temperature is necessary for sperm to be produced. The making of sperm, or the male seed, is very different from egg production in females. Sperm are made continuously in the testes after puberty. Millions of sperm are produced. Each sperm looks a little like a tadpole, the head containing the genetic material and the moving tail allowing the sperm to swim. The sperm are minute. Each sperm is 1/25 of a millimeter long!

Sperm have to be able to swim in order to find their target, the egg. Only healthy active sperm will achieve this. Millions of sperm are released during ejaculation. Ejaculation is the release of sperm-containing fluid (semen) from the penis, which occurs during sexual intercourse or masturbation.

Semen analysis

A man's production of sperm can be checked by examining a sample of semen. The ejaculated semen is looked at under a microscope. The sperm are counted and examined to check that they appear normal and that they are active and swim well. This is called semen analysis.

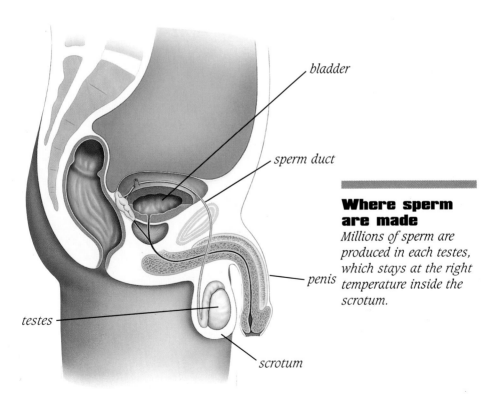

bladder

sperm duct

penis

testes

scrotum

Where sperm are made

Millions of sperm are produced in each testes, which stays at the right temperature inside the scrotum.

During sexual intercourse semen is ejaculated from the end of the penis into the vagina of the female. The sperm then start their journey to meet the egg.

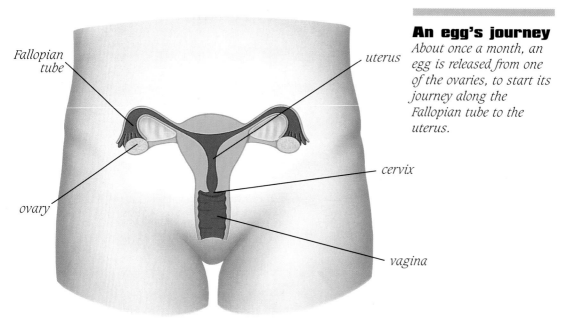

Fallopian tube

uterus

ovary

cervix

vagina

An egg's journey

About once a month, an egg is released from one of the ovaries, to start its journey along the Fallopian tube to the uterus.

Egg Production

Unlike a male who begins producing sperm starting in puberty, a girl is born with all the eggs she will ever need in life. The eggs were produced while the baby girl was developing in her mother's uterus. The number of eggs available to mature is about 40,000—a small number compared with the millions of sperm produced by the male.

Ovaries are the female equivalent of the testes, but lie inside the pelvis, at the base of the abdomen. Girls have two ovaries, one on each side. The eggs sit in the ovaries, dormant or "asleep," until puberty and the start of periods. The pattern of a girl's periods is called the menstrual cycle. This pattern repeats itself every month. First, one egg starts to ripen in one of the ovaries. Halfway through the time from one period to the next, this egg is released from the ovary. This release is called ovulation. The egg is then swept up by the fluffy (technically known as the fimbriat) end of the Fallopian tube.

Other things take place in a girl's body at ovulation. The lining of the womb (technically known as the uterus) starts to get thicker. This is in preparation for pregnancy. If the egg is fertilized, it will attach itself to the inside wall of the uterus, where it will grow during pregnancy. The thickened lining of the uterus makes it more possible for the fertilized egg to attach. Also, at ovulation, the mucus or jelly-like substance in the cervix gets thinner. This makes it easier for the sperm to swim through the cervix to meet the egg.

If the egg is not fertilized by a man's sperm and pregnancy does not take place, then about two weeks after ovulation the body begins to break down the lining of the uterus because it is not needed to nourish a baby. The blood-thickened lining of the uterus is shed and it leaves the body through the vagina. This is called menstruation, or a "period," and the process lasts normally from 3 to 5 days. Then the cycle begins again.

Period pain

It is normal for periods to cause some pain, called "cramps." If taking a painkiller and/or holding a hot-water bottle against the pain does not bring relief, a doctor can offer other solutions.

Hormones

For the female reproductive system to work properly, it is vital that hormones be produced in the ovaries. Hormones are chemicals that travel from the place where they are produced (in this case the ovary) to take a message to another part of the body (in this case the uterus). The ovary always produces estrogen, the main female hormone. At ovulation, or the release of the egg from the ovary, a gap is left in the ovary. This becomes known as the corpus luteum (Latin for "yellow body") as it looks yellow within the ovary. The corpus luteum is a hormone-making factory. It now starts making progesterone, the other female hormone. Progesterone is responsible for thickening the lining of the uterus to let the fertilized egg attach.

Fertilization, or Egg Meets Sperm

During sexual intercourse, sperm are ejaculated into the top part of the female vagina. Luckily, the sperm have very mobile tails and so they are able to swim through the cervix and up through the uterus to try to meet the egg. Meanwhile the egg has no way of propelling itself. It has been swept up by the fimbriate end of the fallopian tube and is drifting down toward the uterus. For fertilization to take place, the sperm must meet the egg in the fallopian tube. The head of the swimming sperm attaches itself to the egg. This is the process of fertilization. The two parts of genetic material join and then the resulting cell is able to start dividing to begin the process of making a baby.

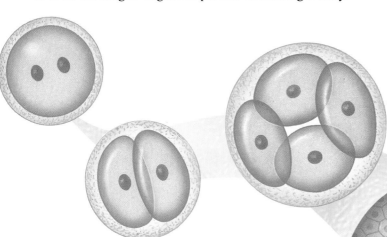

Dividing cells
After fertilization, the single cell starts to divide, making two, then four, then eight, then sixteen cells, and so on. See page 14 for how the cells become a baby.

How Does a Woman Know that She is Pregnant?

When the woman's egg has been fertilized by the man's sperm, things start to change in the woman's body. More and more of the hormone progesterone is released, and the thickened lining of the uterus allows the fertilized egg—now called the embryo—to attach itself. Once attached, the embryo can start to grow and develop into a baby by getting nutrients and oxygen directly from the blood of its mother.

The uterus and growing embryo need a continuous supply of progesterone at the start of pregnancy, to let the pregnancy progress. To ensure this supply, the uterus, at the site of implantation, produces another hormone—HCG or Human Chorionic Gonadotrophin. This tells the ovary to keep producing enough progesterone to maintain the pregnancy.

The effect of all this hormonal activity is that ovulation, or the release of the egg from the ovary, stops. As a result, usually the first thing that most women notice after they have conceived (the egg has been fertilized by the sperm so that the woman is now pregnant) is that they miss a period. Very occasionally, some women may have a small amount of light bleeding, called spotting, at the time they expect a period. But, for most women, menstruation stops when they become pregnant.

Influences
Powerful feelings, a party atmosphere, and alcohol all influence our actions.

Gemma and Jim

Jim and Gemma, who are both 16, have been going out for several months. At the last party they went to, things got out of hand and one thing led to another. They had sex, but they had both been drinking and so it was all over rather quickly and Gemma didn't remember much the next day. Now she is in a panic. Her period is late and for the last couple of years her periods have been regular. She doesn't feel right. She keeps feeling sick, her breasts are sore, and her bra feels too tight. What does she do next? Can she talk to Jim about it? Perhaps if she doesn't think about it, it will go away. But she could be pregnant.

Since Gemma's period is late, it is possible that she is pregnant. If she is, then the high levels of progesterone will be causing changes in her body. She may notice:

- nausea or vomiting ("throwing up"). This is called "morning sickness," but women can feel or be sick at any time of day when they are pregnant.

- breast changes. The breasts are larger and become tender to the touch. This is the start of the process of producing milk for breast-feeding the baby.

- urinary frequency. Most women need to urinate more often during pregnancy.

- constipation. Higher levels of progesterone may make it more difficult for a woman to have a bowel movement.

- feeling tired. This is very common in early pregnancy.

- vaginal discharge. This is an increased loss of clear fluid from the vagina, causing staining on underwear or maybe needing a pad. The discharge occurs because the vaginal lining has also been stimulated by the pregnancy hormones to thicken and to produce more fluid.

Morning sickness
In early pregnancy, a woman may feel sick or vomit.

The symptoms Gemma is experiencing could mean that she is pregnant. But pregnancy can only be determined by medical tests. It is important that she go to a doctor as soon as possible. Then she can get a pregnancy test, which will tell her whether or not she is really pregnant.

The Pregnancy Test

A pregnancy test confirms whether someone is pregnant or not. A woman can have a pregnancy test which tests her urine or her blood. The test works by checking whether the hormone HCG is present in the woman's urine or blood. If no HCG is present, the result will be negative and it means that the woman is not pregnant. If HCG is present, the result will be positive and it means that the woman is pregnant.

Pregnancy tests are very easy to perform. Often women do their own tests at home (urine only). Tests involve either collecting a sample of urine in a clean container and dipping the test strip into it, or holding the test strip in a stream of urine as you go to the bathroom. The urine passes along the test strip to two windows. If the test has worked, a colored line or dot will appear in the smaller window. This is called the control. The test is positive if a colored mark then appears also in the large window. This confirms the presence of HCG.

Pregnancy tests (urine only) can be bought at a pharmacy, or can be arranged for you at a family planning clinic or a doctor's office. If you do choose to do your own pregnancy test, it is important that you follow the directions very carefully. It is always wise to go to a medical professional as well so that you can be sure that your results are accurate.

A positive test
A pink mark has appeared in the second window, showing the woman that she is pregnant.

How Long Does Pregnancy Last?

The date that the baby is due is calculated from the date of the first day of the woman's last menstrual period. Pregnancy lasts 40 weeks from that date. Not all babies are born on exactly the calculated date, but 90 percent of women deliver between one week before and one week after that date.

2 Pregnancy
How the Baby Develops

Pregnancy is amazing and wonderful. At conception, the female egg is fertilized by the male sperm. From this single fertilized egg, a human baby is formed.

How the Fertilized Egg Becomes a Baby

After fertilization in the fallopian tube, the egg starts to divide, making two cells, forming what is called a zygote. The zygote then divides and makes four cells, then eight cells, then sixteen cells, and so on. This cell multiplication continues during the journey along the fallopian tube to the uterus. By the time the one hundred cell stage is reached, it is called an embryo and is ready to implant, or attach, itself to the lining of the uterus.

The embryo forms an attachment to the lining of the uterus, which will become the placenta. The placenta is a mass of blood vessels attached to the developing baby by the umbilical cord. The umbilical cord is the "lifeline" from the mother to the embryo. It is attached to the baby at one end of the cord, and is also attached to the placenta at the other end of the cord. The placenta passes oxygen and nutrients directly from the mother's blood to the embryo through the umbilical cord, so that the embryo can grow.

As the embryo implants into the uterus lining, a sac starts to develop around the embryo. This will become the fluid-filled amniotic sac, which will surround the baby and provide it with a safe growing environment. The amniotic fluid in the sac cushions and protects the embryo while it grows and develops inside the uterus.

8–9 weeks old
At this stage the baby is about two-thirds of an inch long (17 mm) from head to bottom.
It is floating in the amniotic sac and is attached to the placenta (top left) by the umbilical cord.

The First Twelve Weeks

Implantation takes place about two weeks after fertilization. However, pregnancy is normally calculated from the first day of the woman's last menstrual period. So implantation occurs about four weeks after that date. During the next eight weeks the baby will continue to develop from the 100-cell embryo. All the parts of the baby's body will be formed from these original identical cells.

The first parts of the baby to form are the brain and spinal cord and the heart. By six weeks, the baby's heart can be seen beating on an ultrasound scan (see page 20). The arms and legs start to develop, and then the features of the face—ears, eyes, mouth, etc. After development of the upper part of the arms and legs, development begins of the feet and hands. At the same time, all the internal organs— heart, brain, lungs, kidneys, liver and stomach—are continuing to form. By 12 to 14 weeks of pregnancy the baby is fully formed.

The greatest damage to a baby can occur during these first 12 weeks of pregnancy. The use of drugs, the use of alcohol, or an infection can cause damage to the baby's development. Sometimes it is not possible to tell what has caused the damage. Damage to the developing baby is known as congenital deformity.

For example, if the heart does not develop normally, babies can be born with congenital heart disease. If development of the spinal cord is abnormal, spina bifida may result. If damage occurs at the time that the face is developing, it may not form normally and the baby may be born with a cleft of the lip and palate.

Thalidomide

In the early 1960s, a drug called thalidomide was commonly given to pregnant women to help treat pregnancy sickness. The drug damaged babies at the phase at which the arms & legs were developing and caused major limb deformities.

The Baby Becomes Viable

At 12 weeks, the developing baby is now called a fetus. After 12 to 14 weeks, the fetus starts to grow fast. All the finer features of the baby start to form, such as eyebrows and eyelashes, fingernails, and toenails. Between 16 and 18 weeks, the mother often starts to feel the baby moving in the womb. Initially it just feels like little flutterings but, as the weeks pass, the movements (kicks) get stronger.

After 24 weeks, the fetus is known as viable. This means that, if it were born at this stage, it would be developed enough to have a chance of survival. It would obviously need a great deal of medical care to survive, but all of the organs of the body are developed well enough to make survival outside the womb a possibility. A baby born at this stage is still very immature. For example, the baby's eyes do not open until 26 weeks.

Intensive care

Prematurely born babies need intensive hospital care to enable them to develop and gain strength as they would have done in the mother's womb.

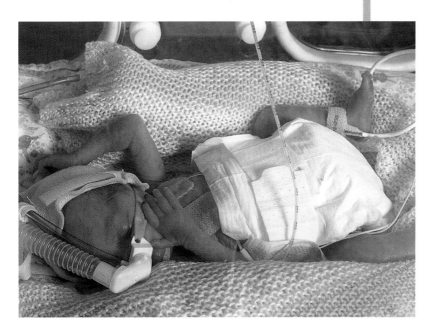

At about 32 weeks, the baby starts to settle into the position in the uterus from which it will be born. Most babies are born head first, but occasionally the baby settles into a position with its feet pointing downwards. Birth from this position is called a breech delivery.

Pregnancy Problems

During the early weeks, things can go so wrong that the pregnancy fails and miscarriage occurs. The woman may notice bleeding from the vagina and will often then start to feel cramping abdominal pains. The doctor will probably arrange an ultrasound scan and, if it is not possible to see a beating fetal heart, then it is assumed that the fetus has died. Occasionally, the miscarriage will complete naturally—i.e. all the contents of the uterus are lost in the vaginal bleeding. Sometimes, to prevent excessive blood loss, the woman needs a brief operation to remove the contents of the uterus.

Sometimes the fertilized egg or embryo continues to grow in the Fallopian tube, instead of moving down and implanting in the uterus. This is known as an ectopic pregnancy and is potentially very dangerous for the mother. A damaged tube, or getting pregnant while using an IUD for contraception, increases the risk of an ectopic pregnancy.

Prenatal Care

This is the care given to women during pregnancy. (Prenatal means "before birth.") The aim of prenatal care is to ensure that the mother remains healthy throughout the pregnancy and that the baby develops normally. In the past, pregnancy was a dangerous time for women. Many women died from the complications of pregnancy, and the risks to the baby were also high. This remains the case in the developing world today. In the developed world, with better health and nutrition and improved care during pregnancy, the risks have reduced dramatically.

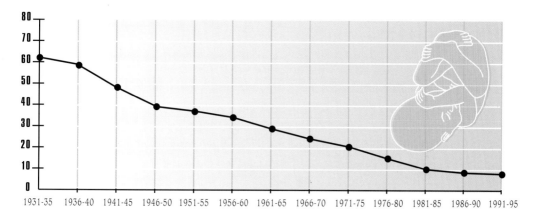

A number of professionals share the care of women during pregnancy. Midwives are nurses specially trained to take care of pregnant women prenatally, during delivery, and for a short time after the birth (postnatally). The family doctor will also participate in this care and will continue to look after mother and baby after birth. Obstetricians are doctors who specialize in dealing with pregnancy. They are trained to deal with any complications that may arise during pregnancy or delivery.

Care during the first half of pregnancy is taken to help the mother decide where she wants to have the baby—in a hospital, birthing center, or at home. Most women choose to have their babies in a hospital, and choose an obstetrician to assist them in the delivery. During the first half of pregnancy, medical professionals also help the mother decide if she wants to have prenatal tests to look for abnormalities in the baby's growth.

Prenatal tests

Prenatal tests check for babies with Down's syndrome, spina bifida, and other structural abnormalities. If abnormalities are found, couples can be offered termination of pregnancy.

Women can be offered blood tests or special types of scans, to check the risk of their baby's being affected. If the risk is found to be very high, then other tests, such as amniocentesis can be offered to confirm whether the baby is affected. Amniocentesis involves passing a needle into the amniotic fluid in the uterus, withdrawing some fluid, and then testing it.

A worrying decision

Joe and Ann are expecting their first baby. They have been offered tests to be sure their baby is not suffering from Down's syndrome or spina bifida. Ann had a blood test done at the sixteenth week of pregnancy and she has just found out that the test is positive. She knows that this means that her baby has a higher chance of being affected by one of these problems, but the only way she can be certain is by having an amniocentesis. She is very frightened about this. She knows there is a possibility that she will have a miscarriage because the test involves putting a needle into the amniotic sac. She doesn't like needles and is scared for her baby. She is also very nervous about finding out the result of the test. She and Joe are still uncertain about whether they would want to terminate the pregnancy if the test shows that the baby is affected. It is a very scary time for them.

A midwife describes her work

When I first meet a woman at the start of her pregnancy, I explain about the care she will have. There are blood tests to arrange to make sure that she is healthy. She then has important decisions to make about whether she wants to have tests done to check that her developing baby is normal. I tell her that the tests are available in the first half of pregnancy and that, if she finds that her baby is affected, it would be possible to offer an abortion. I must also tell her about ultrasound scans. These are a safe way of looking at the baby during pregnancy. Later in the pregnancy I will see the woman more often to check her own health and that the baby is growing well.

It's also my job to prepare women for childbirth and the arrival of their new baby. I do this with individual women and in classes. We discuss feelings about pregnancy, how to feed the baby, what you need when the baby arrives, and all sorts of other useful things.

When a woman goes into labor, I'm there to help her, to check that she stays well and that the baby's heartbeat is healthy despite the stress of labor. Then the really exciting part starts when I guide the woman through the process of delivering her baby into the world. The baby's first cry and the woman's relief at the end of labor are really moving.

Listening in

The midwife can check the baby's heartbeat by listening through a simple funnel.

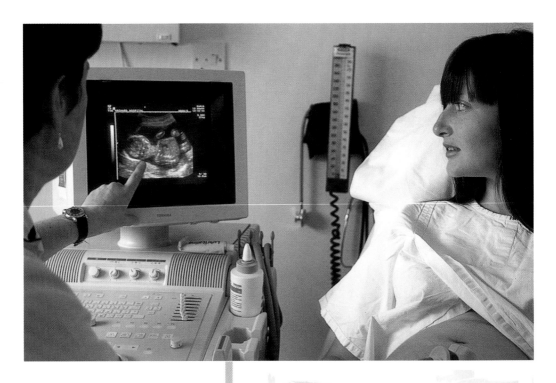

Having a scan

Some warmed gel rubbed on the woman's stomach helps the scanning instrument to make good contact and get a clear picture of the inside of the uterus.

In the second half of pregnancy, the aim of prenatal care is to make sure that the woman stays well. This means picking up any pregnancy-related problems such as high blood pressure. The health of the growing baby is also monitored. The size of the uterus is checked to make sure the baby is growing, the baby's heart is listened to, and the mother is asked how lively the baby is in the uterus. Monitoring the baby's kicks is a good way of checking that it is healthy.

The ultrasound scan

An ultrasound scan is a test using soundwaves to build up an image of the baby in the uterus. The test is safe to mother and baby, and research continues to check the safety of the test.

The test

- *checks measurements and growth of the baby*
- *checks whether there is more than one baby in the uterus*
- *detects abnormalities of parts of the baby, e.g. the face and spine*
- *shows the position of the placenta*

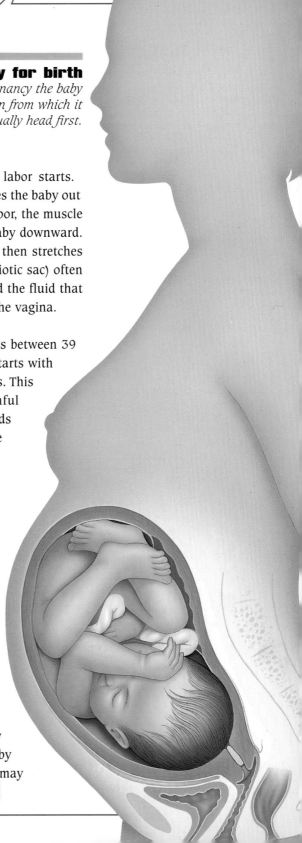

Ready for birth
*At the end of pregnancy the baby
settles into the position from which it
will be be born—usually head first.*

Delivery

When it is time for the baby to be born, labor starts.
Labor is the means by which the body pushes the baby out
of the uterus and through the vagina. In labor, the muscle
wall of the uterus contract and push the baby downward.
The long tube of the cervix flattens, thins, then stretches
open. The membranes (the wall of the amniotic sac) often
rupture. This means that the sac bursts and the fluid that
was inside it then trickles or gushes from the vagina.

For the vast majority of women, labor starts between 39
and 41 weeks after conception. It usually starts with
the onset of regular and painful contractions. This
means that the woman feels painful
tightenings of the uterus, followed by periods
of relaxation. The contractions become
stronger and more frequent as labor
progresses. Labor lasts, on average,
between six and twelve hours.

When the cervix has dilated, or opened
fully, the woman gets the urge to push.
The doctor or midwife will tell the
woman about how and when to push. If
necessary, small incisions, or tiny cuts,
are made so that the vagina does not
tear during delivery.

Once the baby's head is outside of the
vagina, its body follows quickly and
easily. As soon as the baby is born, the
umbilical cord which has attached the baby
to the placenta is clamped and cut. The baby
is then passed to its mother to cuddle. She may

also wish to put the baby to her breast for a first feeding.

Sometimes the baby is a little slow taking its first breath and may need some help. The nose and mouth are cleaned out and the baby can be given some oxygen.

After the birth of the baby, the placenta (sometimes known as the afterbirth) must be delivered.

Difficulties With Labor

Sometimes labor does not start at the right time. If the woman has not started labor within a week or two after her due date, then labor is induced, or assisted along by giving drugs to stimulate the uterus to contract. If problems occur during pregnancy, such as poor growth of the baby, then labor may be induced early.

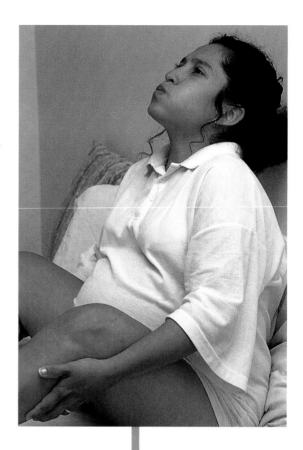

Labor
Breathing exercises help make the pain of labor easier to cope with. Pregnant women are taught these exercises as part of their prenatal care.

Sometimes, at the end of labor, the contractions are not strong enough to push the baby out. It can be helped by using forceps or Ventouse (a vacuum extraction device). These are applied to the baby's head and the obstetrician then pulls the baby out.

Sometimes the obstetrician recommends that the baby be born by Caesarian section. This is an operation in which a cut is made through the skin of the abdomen and then through the muscle of the uterus and the baby is delivered through the opening. The operation is sometimes planned, or may be needed as an emergency during labor if things are not progressing normally.

Postnatal Care

During the first few days after delivery, the new mother must recover from the physical stress of labor and must get to know her new baby. She is confronted with many experiences for the first time. Most important, she must learn how to feed her baby.

During the first few days after delivery, blood is lost from the vagina as the area where the placenta was attached starts to heal. The uterus contracts from its large size (extending up to the woman's ribs at the end of pregnancy) to its normal size (about the size of a small pear).

The woman is very tired after the physical stress of labor, and the baby is also making many physical and emotional demands. Many women (about 80 percent) experience the "baby blues." Around the third or fourth day after delivery they may feel very down and tearful and are easily upset. These feelings usually end quickly, helped by the support of the woman's partner and family. However, for about 10 percent of women, the feelings continue, and coping with the baby becomes very difficult. This is known as postpartum depression. The causes of it are not fully understood, but family doctors, and health care professionals are very aware of the problem and offer support and treatment for women who become depressed.

The woman, her partner, and the baby are now a new family and are embarking upon the pleasures, excitement, trials, and tribulations of family life for many years to come!

A family
A baby brings fun and excitement as well as constant work!

3 Take Care of Yourself!
Protecting Your Fertility

Fertility refers to a woman's ability to become pregnant or a man's ability to get a woman pregnant. The way you live can affect your ability to get pregnant in the future and to carry a pregnancy successfully. The influence of lifestyle on fertility applies to both women and men.

The life you lead now as a teen affects your future, so remember to make positive choices that maintain and protect your health. For males, sperm production can be reduced by excessive alcohol consumption, by cigarette smoking, and by recreational drug use. Anabolic steroids, which are used illegally by some athletes to enhance their performance, also suppress sperm production. Similarly, some treatments prescribed by doctors (for instance, for cancer) can reduce the number of sperm produced. Some men are exposed to toxins in their work place that may adversely affect their future fertility.

Sperm production can also be affected by damage to the testes. Damage can occur by physical injury—for example, falling astride the crossbar of a bike, can cause trauma to the testes. Equally, damage can be caused by some infections. The most notable of these is mumps, if the mumps virus infects the testes.

For females, using recreational drugs, smoking to excess, and being overweight are all factors that can result in reduced fertility. This means that it can be more difficult to get pregnant when you want to. There are circumstances in

Alcohol
Drinking alcohol might seem a "macho" thing to do, but drinking to excess can lead to a reduced sperm count.

women's lives that keep the ovarian cycle from working normally, thereby stopping ovulation and periods. Many girls with eating disorders who lose excessive amounts of weight find that their periods stop. Similarly, girls training as professional athletes may find that the rigors of the training program halt the ovarian cycle, and their periods stop.

"I've just got engaged and when we're married, I'd really love for us to have kids. I just hope that all the stress when I was a teenager hasn't affected my chances. I was anorexic and my weight fell to about seventy pounds, and I don't think I had any periods for two or three years."
(Kathryn, age 25)

The use of alcohol and drugs can lead to other behaviors that put young people at risk. Alcohol and drugs can reduce inhibitions and lead people more easily into casual sexual relationships. This then increases their risk of catching a sexually transmitted infection (STI).

Recreational drug use is illegal and expensive. To raise the funds to maintain their drug habit, some young people of both sexes become involved in prostitution—so putting themselves at risk of infection and pregnancy.

Sexually Transmitted Infections

Sexually transmitted infections (STIs) are infections that are passed during oral, anal, or penile-vaginal (penis to vagina) sexual contact. There are many STIs, and often when people are infected with them, they do not have any symptoms. Some, like chlamydia and gonorrhea, can be cured by taking medicine. Others, like genital warts, herpes, and the human immunodeficiency virus (HIV), cannot be cured.

Some STIs can cause infertility. For example, in women, an untreated chlamydia infection can result in the blockage of Fallopian tubes (the route that the egg has to take from the ovary to the uterus); this is a very common cause of infertility. In men, chlamydial infection can reduce the activity levels of sperm, which reduces the chances of the sperm being able to fertilize the egg. Chlamydia is the most common STI among the teenage population. Various studies from Western Europe have shown that up to 20 percent of women ages 15 to 19 may be infected with chlamydia. Both male and female teenagers are at risk for chlamydia, as well as other STIs. In fact, each year one out of every four teens will get an STI.

Gonorrhea

Gonorrhea is another STI which can cause problems similar to chlamydia. Sexually active teens are most at risk for this STI. There is a 50 percent chance of being infected with gonorrhea if a teen has sex just one time with an infected partner.

Lucy's test results

Hi, I'm Lucy. I've just had a real shock. Lee, my boyfriend, told me last week that he had these spots on his penis. He'd seen his doctor and he's been told he has warts. He also said he had to tell me, because I ought to have a check-up. I psyched myself up to go to one of those clinics that deal with sexually transmitted diseases. I found a hot line in one of my magazines and they told me how to arrange it. So I went. I didn't enjoy the experience, but I suppose it was okay. The bad news is that the swab for chlamydia came back positive, so I've had to have treatment. They took my first Pap smear. They told me that we all should have those and they check for cancer of the cervix. What's even worse is that they have found wart virus in that smear, so I'll have to keep having that repeated to check.

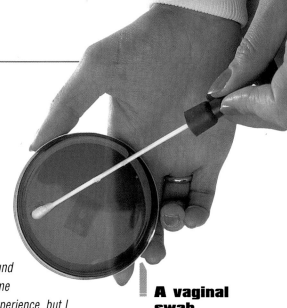

A vaginal swab

AIDS

This baby with AIDS was born in Cambodia, a country with a very high rate of HIV infection.

Research has shown that teens who have had an STI are at higher risk for contracting the HIV virus (the virus that causes AIDS) and Hepatitis B. Unfortunately, STDs don't occur in isolation. People with one infection are likely to have other infections too. The other serious infections that can be acquired at the same time are hepatitis B and the HIV virus. These are both transmitted sexually. People usually do not know that they have the infection until many months or even years later. Many people who catch one of these viruses will become life-long carriers of it. It will never leave their bodies. Since most people do not know they are carriers, unless they have had special blood tests to prove it, they continue to spread the virus to other people by unprotected sexual contact. Women carriers can pass the HIV virus to their babies when they are pregnant. Up to 25 percent of the babies born to HIV-positive mothers are born infected by the virus and are unlikely to survive until adulthood.

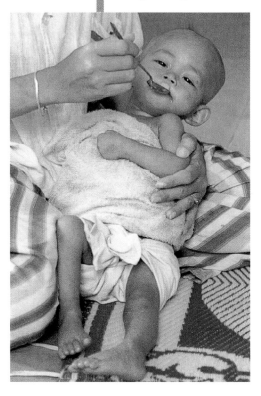

Positive Thinking

On a more positive note, there are things a couple can do to take care of themselves and their baby when they are planning pregnancy. In order to enhance their chances of getting pregnant, and of having a healthy pregnancy, women are advised to:

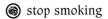

- stop smoking
- reduce the amount of alcohol they drink
- aim for their ideal weight
- check that their rubella (German measles) immunity is adequate
- take extra folic acid (both before getting pregnant and for the first 12 weeks of pregnancy).

Rubella is a childhood infectious disease causing a rash and fever for a few days. But, if a pregnant woman catches rubella in the early weeks of pregnancy, she may lose the baby. If not, the baby is very likely to be born with the congenital rubella syndrome. Babies affected by congenital rubella syndrome suffer from deafness, blindness, heart abnormalities, and mental handicap. Immunization against rubella (which prevents you from catching it) has dramatically reduced the number of babies born with this syndrome. Young women can check that their immunization has been successful by having a blood test.

Rubella
A newborn baby with congenital rubella syndrome.

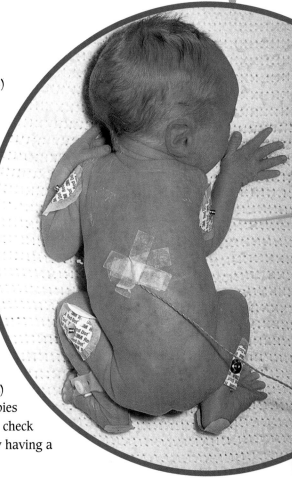

Taking extra folic acid (one of the B vitamins) helps prevent neural tube defects in babies. The most common of these defects is spina bifida, an exposed section of the spinal cord in the lower back of the baby. The cord becomes damaged, leaving the child paralyzed from the waist down.

A high risk of pregnancy

Danielle (16) and Tony (18) have both left school but do not have regular jobs. They have been going out together for six months. They go to clubs in town and have a good time drinking and dancing. Drugs are readily available if you know who to talk to and you have the cash. Danielle knows that Tony and his friends break into cars and steal the radio equipment. It is easy to sell this. So Tony usually does have cash for cannabis or ecstasy. During the day, they find life is pretty boring. They occasionally have part-time work in the grocery store. But, to pass the time, they both smoke about 20 cigarettes a day. They started having sex early in their relationship. Danielle is on the pill, but often forgets to take it. Tony refuses to use condoms. They have both had sexual partners before. Tony had sex with men when he was younger. He was already into drugs when he was 15 and an older man found him partners who would pay him for sex. Danielle is at high risk for pregnancy and getting a STI. Danielle and Tony's lifestyles are putting their health at great risk and could also greatly affect the health of a baby.

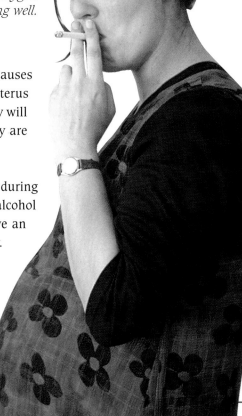

Smoking during pregnancy

When you smoke, nicotine and carbon monoxide get into your blood. This reduces the supply of oxygen to your baby and keeps it from growing well.

Why Avoid Smoking, Alcohol, and Drugs?

It is well known that smoking while pregnant causes problems. The baby will not grow as well in the uterus and there is also a much higher chance that the baby will be born prematurely (too early). The risks to a baby are greater if it is both underweight and premature.

If a woman consumes a large volume of alcohol during pregnancy, her baby can be born with the fetal alcohol syndrome. Babies with this problem are small, have an odd facial appearance, and fail to develop normally.

Cannabis used during pregnancy does not seem to affect the growth of the baby. However, there is evidence that when these babies are toddlers, they perform less well than those whose mothers did not use cannabis in pregnancy.

If a pregnant woman uses heroin, it crosses the placenta and affects the baby. Some days after birth, these babies experience withdrawal effects from the heroin they have been used to. They become irritable and have difficulties with breathing and feeding. They are effectively heroin addicts at birth. During the period of withdrawal the baby is often very ill and may need intensive care.

Infections

Infections caught by a mother during pregnancy can upset the well-being of the baby in the uterus.

- Infections caught from other people (e.g. chicken pox or German measles) can infect the baby, causing damage to it.
- Infections caught from animals can harm the baby. The organism Toxoplasma is found in the feces of cats. If this infection is caught by a woman during pregnancy, it can seriously damage the fetus. Sheep themselves can miscarry or give birth to sick lambs after infection with an organism called Listeria. If a woman handles infected sheep during lambing, she too can miscarry.
- Infections can be caught from the food that we eat. Toxoplasma can be found in raw meat. Salmonella is found in raw eggs. Listeria is often found in soft cheeses such as Brie and blue cheeses, pâté and cooked-chilled meals. To avoid infection, it is very important that such meals are properly reheated.
- Sexually transmitted infections such as hepatitis B and HIV can be transmitted directly to the baby in the uterus, and the baby will be born infected by the virus.

Heroin
Heroin use is increasingly common in people aged under 25 years.

4 Teenage Pregnancy Figures and Facts

Why Do Teenagers Get Pregnant?

Many studies about teenage pregnancy and parenthood have been performed in both Europe and the United States. It seems that most teenage pregnancies are unplanned, perhaps as many as 85 percent each year in the United States. But there are variations. For example, among some ethnic groups and cultures, it is the accepted norm to marry and start a family before you are 20 years old.

Certain factors can make a teenager more "at risk" for teen pregnancy and teenage parenthood. However, any person

Births per 1,000 women ages 15–19

The U.S. has the highest teen pregnancy rate in the developed world—twice as high as England and Canada, and nine times as high as the Netherlands.

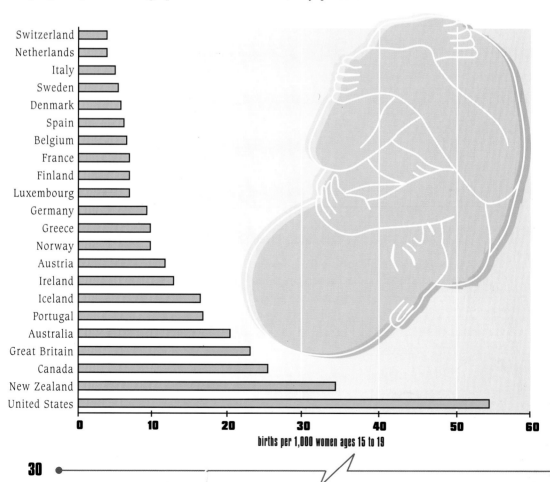

births per 1,000 women ages 15 to 19

who is sexually active can become pregnant or get their partner pregnant.

Research studies have shown that certain life situations make some teens more likely to become teen parents. Children whose parents were teenage parents are at higher risk for repeating the cycle and becoming parents themselves. Teenagers who have dropped out of school or are excluded from education are also at higher risk for pregnancy. Teenagers who come from low income or socially disadvantaged backgrounds are also at higher risk for teen pregnancy.

Teenagers who have been sexually abused are also at greater risk for becoming pregnant while still a teen. In addition, teenagers who experience low self esteem are also at greater risk for teen pregnancy. But remember, just because a person may be more "at risk" for teen pregnancy due to their life situation, it does not mean that they always become teenage parents. Unprotected sex can result in pregnancy for any teenager, no matter what life situation they experience.

International Statistics

The rate of teenage pregnancy varies widely from country to country. There have also been large differences over time between countries. In Denmark, the number of births to women ages 15 to 19 has declined greatly from 40 per 1,000 in 1966 to well under 10 per 1,000 since the early 1980s. In the United States, the number of births to women age 15 to 19 started to rise in the late 1980s and peaked at over 112 in 1992. Why is there such a difference between countries that in many ways are very similar?

Getting pregnant— the truth

You may hear some myths about things that help avoid pregnancy. Myths are not true! The facts are:

1. *It is easy to get pregnant the first time you have sex.*

2. *Of teenagers who have unprotected sex, 90 percent of them will be pregnant within one year.*

3. *Girls can still get pregnant when they think they are menstruating (having a period).*

4. *You can get pregnant if you have sex standing up.*

5. *Girls do not have to have an orgasm to get pregnant.*

6. *If the boy pulls his penis out of the vagina just before he ejaculates, it is still possible to get pregnant. Some sperm may have been released into the vagina before ejaculation.*

7. *It can also be possible to get pregnant even if the boy ejaculates outside but very close to the vagina. Sperm are strong swimmers!*

It seems that the countries that have been most successful in lowering the rate of teenage pregnancy have some characteristics in common:

- good sex education in schools, so that young people learn fact and not myth and learn about sex in the context of relationships
- teenagers feel more confident and assertive so they delay the start of sexual activity
- good education and job prospects for young people
- family attitudes about discussing sex are open. Teenagers find it easy to talk to their parents and other family members about sex and relationships.

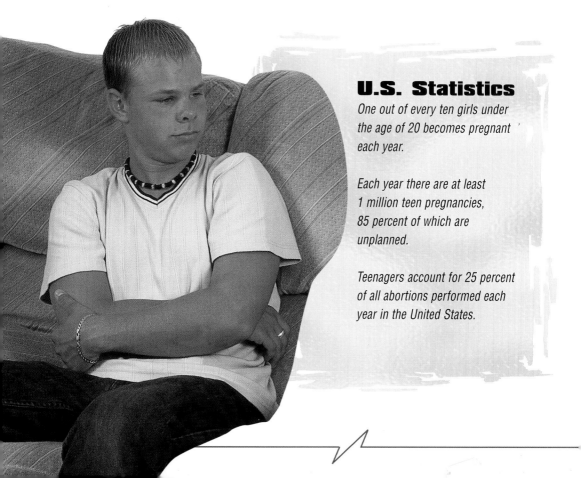

U.S. Statistics

One out of every ten girls under the age of 20 becomes pregnant each year.

Each year there are at least 1 million teen pregnancies, 85 percent of which are unplanned.

Teenagers account for 25 percent of all abortions performed each year in the United States.

"A baby is for keeps"

Mary-Jo and Craig are both 14 when Mary-Jo discovers that she is pregnant. What will they decide to do? Are they ready to become parents? There are so many things that they should think about. The end result of pregnancy is the arrival of a baby. What does that mean in reality? Babies have many needs, including:

Love and affection, ideally from both parents

Will Craig stay around throughout Mary-Jo's pregnancy, even though she will not always be able to go out with him? Will he be there in the hospital when the baby is born? Will Mary-Jo and Craig together, be able to give the love that the baby will need all through childhood? After all, it will start school before they are 20.

Feeding. Babies need to be fed, and very often. Some women breastfeed, while others choose to feed the baby formula that is bought at the store.

How will Mary-Jo feel about feeding her baby? How will Craig support her? Babies need to be fed during the night as well as the day. How will they cope with getting up at night to feed the baby?

To be kept dry and clean. Babies have no control over their bowels or bladder. Their skin is very sensitive. If it is left in contact with urine or feces, it will become red and sore. In order to prevent this, babies need regular changing of their diapers. Most people nowadays in Europe and in the United States use disposable diapers. Others use cloth diapers that can be washed and reused.

Newborn babies may need 6 to 10 clean diapers every day! Will Craig and Mary-Jo be able to make diaper-changing time fun and a time to get to know their baby? How will they afford to buy the endless supply of new diapers that they will need?

Care. Babies and children are dependent on their parents for all their needs until they themselves are adults. These needs include a warm, safe home, clothing, food, and education. They cannot be left unattended.

How will Craig and Mary-Jo feel about the restriction that their baby will impose on their social life? It will not be easy for them to go out together after the baby is born. Meanwhile, their friends will still be going to clubs and having a good time.

?

What's wrong?
Babies and very young children cannot tell us what is upsetting them.

Attention when it cries. Newborn babies are able to do very little other than sleep, eat, and cry. It can be very difficult to figure out why a baby is crying. The list of possible reasons is endless. The baby may be hungry. It may be uncomfortable because it has a wet or dirty diaper. It may be too hot or too cold. It may have gas or colic. It may be tired but unable to sleep. It may be bored and wanting to play, or lonely and wanting company.

What will Craig and Mary-Jo feel like when their baby cries and won't stop? How will they manage?

Attention when the baby is sick. Babies and young children are often sick. They easily catch infections from other young children. It can be very frightening when your child suddenly becomes sick.

How will Mary-Jo and Craig cope in this situation? Will they know how to get help?

Is Being Pregnant as a Teenager Good for You?

There are risks attached to being pregnant at any age, but the risks are greater for the very young or for those at the end of the reproductive life. Pregnancy problems are more common in teenage pregnancies. These include high blood pressure and the risk of a dangerous illness called eclampsia. Prolonged or difficult labor is more common for teens, particularly because teenagers are often not physically fully grown when they get pregnant.

Teenagers are the group most likely to smoke during pregnancy. Of teenagers who are pregnant, two thirds have smoked before getting pregnant and 50 percent continue to smoke through the pregnancy. We have already seen the harmful effects of smoking in pregnancy (see page 28).

Since most teenagers have not planned to be pregnant, few have taken health measures before conceiving and at the very start of pregnancy. For example, very few are taking folic acid supplements (see page 27).

As soon as you know you are pregnant, you must think about whether you want to continue with the pregnancy or choose termination or adoption. You must cope with the idea of being pregnant and consider how to tell your family and friends. If you decide to keep the baby, you must start preparing for parenthood. Many teenagers faced with these dilemmas end up delaying making decisions. Thus, their pregnancy is therefore confirmed much later than in older women who are pregnant. The delays are often the result of not expecting to be pregnant, fear of disapproval, fear that your privacy will not be respected, fear that everyone will tell you to have an abortion, or simply wanting to deny that it is happening to you. As a result, a high proportion of pregnant teenagers do not see their family doctor early in pregnancy and do not have early prenatal care.

Looking ahead
Samantha feels proud to be pregnant. But what will life hold for her and her baby?

Depression

Postpartum depression (see page 23) is three times more common after giving birth while still a teenager. Four out of every ten young mothers will be affected.

Social Problems

Teenage parents are more likely to face obstacles than teens who are not parents. Teenage parents are more likely to live in poverty and be unemployed. Teenage mothers earn half the lifetime income of women who have children in their 20s. Teenage parents are also less likely to complete their education and training.

Relationships that start when you are a teenager have a higher chance of breaking up than the relationships you form when you are older. In a British study, 50 percent of teenage mothers were no longer with the father of their baby one year after the baby's birth. Having a baby puts an extra stress on a relationship.

Teenagers worry about their housing when they get pregnant. Some are lucky enough to have supportive families who either let them stay in the family home with their baby or help them to live elsewhere. Other teenage parents have trouble finding accommodations that they can afford.

Being a parent while still a young teenager does restrict your social life. Before you go out, you must always think first about how to care for your baby.

But the story does not always have to be one of doom and gloom. There are teenagers, like Cathy, who become excellent parents, who get the support of their families and manage to complete their education and find good jobs.

Children of teenage parents

Babies of teenage mothers are 25 percent more likely than those of older mothers to weigh under 5.5 pounds (2.5 kg) at birth. Being small at birth carries risks to health and well-being.

Death rates for babies of teenage mothers are 60 percent higher than for babies of older mothers.

Death rates for children ages 1 to 3 years are highest if their mother is under 20 years old.

Children of very young parents are more likely to suffer accidents during early childhood.

These young children are twice as likely to be admitted to a hospital after an accident or with an illness than children of older mothers.

Cathy and Amy

Hi, I'm Cathy. I'm 16 now but I had my daughter Amy when I was 13. I was so scared when I thought I was pregnant and I didn't know what my Mom and Dad would say. I knew they would be really disappointed in me. I decided to just keep quiet, and kept hoping my period would come, but it never did. I was pregnant. About six months later, Mom noticed my stomach, because it was pretty big by then. She took me to the doctor, who sent me for a ultrasound scan. And there was my baby. I didn't know whether to shout for joy or cry. Mom was with me and although she was really upset that I had hid everything from her, she stuck by me and talked to Dad. When I went into labor, Mom came with me too. I was so scared! After a long labor, Amy was born and she was just perfect! It was love at first sight.

The first few weeks were tough when I came home. Mom and Dad were great, but I was so tired. I had to keep getting up at night to feed and take care of Amy. Some of my friends thought it was great. Some didn't. Everyone was still doing their own thing, going shopping, going to parties, hanging out, and I couldn't join in.

Going back to school was the hardest part. I'm lucky because my family takes care of Amy while I'm at school so that I can graduate. But it's hard being a teenage parent and going to school at the same time. Doing homework, making Amy's dinner, getting her bathed and ready for bed is really exhausting, but I still love Amy so much. Everything is working out because my family has been so great.

You'll probably notice that I don't mention Amy's dad very much. He left me when I was pregnant. He's really proud to be a dad and sees Amy some weekends, but he's only 16 now and he has a new girlfriend. I'm determined to make something of myself. I wish I hadn't gotten pregnant so young, but then I wouldn't have Amy and she's gorgeous.

Homework

As well as keeping up with her school work, Cathy has started to read and write with Amy.

Changing styles
Schools have almost always taught the biology of sex and reproduction. In 1948 (above) it was remarkable for a class to be able to see a film on the subject. Today, some schools have programmable computer babies, to help students learn aspects of childcare.

Sex Education—The Facts

Good sex education in school, from family, and from other sources helps teenagers to make informed decisions about sexual relationships. There are many programs around the world which aim to help educate young people about their sexuality. The more educated young people are about their sexuality, the more able they are to make informed decisions about when to start having sexual relationships and take action to protect themselves against pregnancy and sexually transmitted infections.

In the Netherlands, for example, sex education is an important part of the school curriculum. It includes not just the scientific descriptions of the biology of sex, but also discussion on morality and ethics. When asked, Dutch teens report being less hesitant to talk to their parents about sex than teenagers in the United States. In addition, Dutch teens also have higher rates of contraceptive use than teens in the United States—85 percent of teenagers in the Netherlands use contraception the first time they have sex, compared with only 78 percent in the United States. As a result of their sex education, Dutch teenagers have one of the lowest rates of conception in the world. They also, on average, delay the start of sexual relationships until they are older. Young men in the Netherlands are also more likely to discuss contraception with their partner.

Other programs have been developed in Great Britain and the United States, particularly in areas of high rates of teenage pregnancy. Some programs use young people to teach others of a similar age. An example is "Teen Advocates" attached to the Bronx Center for Planned Parenthood in New York. There young people are trained to teach others. They use a drama program to engage their audience in program discussion. Being the same age and from the same community, they use language and examples that teenagers can relate to. Teenagers who have seen the presentations seem more able to make decisions about their own sexual health and discuss contraception and other related topics.

"I thought sex ed at school would be terrible. But we had these cool sessions with older kids leading them. I don't feel so hung up about talking about sex and contraception now."

A program used in schools in Devon in England covers awareness of relationships and attitudes toward others and information about sexual relationships and contraception. It is taught partly by teachers and school nurses but, by the age of 14, students are also taught by other teenagers age 16 to 19, who have been through the program themselves. Most students say that they have gained both skills and useful information from the sessions and feel that their sex education has been acceptable.

So, understanding your sexuality can help you make informed choices about your life. It can help you become more confident in your relationships and in your decision making. Knowing the facts can help you decide when to become sexually active, as well as help you take action to protect yourself against pregnancy and sexually transmitted infection.

5 Unwanted Pregnancy
Looking At the Options

Ann's dilemma

Ann, age16, has been worried. Her period is late and she feels sick. She doesn't know much about pregnancy, but she has heard her mother talking with a neighbor, who felt terrible at the beginning of her pregnancy. She has read in her magazines about girls getting pregnant. She doesn't really think that she could be pregnant. She and her boyfriend Nick have only had sex a few times. But neither of them has done much about contraception. Ann had been thinking of asking her friend about how she got the pill.

Pregnancy is not always a straightforward happy event. Many women get pregnant accidentally. For some women and for most teenagers who have not planned to have a baby, the discovery that they are pregnant is frightening.The first thing they need to do is talk to an adult, such as a parent, school counselor, teacher, social worker, nurse, or doctor. The sooner the teenager talks to an adult, the more time the teen has to think about what they would like to do about the pregnancy.

Adoption

Adoption used to be a very common choice for unmarried women who found themselves pregnant. Today, however, fewer teens are choosing adoption and are instead opting to become teen parents. Only 4 percent of pregnant teens choose adoption—that's about 12,000 per year.

If Ann is pregnant, what are her options?

- She can continue with her pregnancy and look after her baby with Nick's help, or on her own, or with the help of her family.
- She can continue with the pregnancy, and when the baby is born, arrange to have an adult family member or another family care for the baby until she is able to do so (temporary foster care).
- She can arrange to have an abortion (termination).

What Is an Abortion?

The word abortion means the ending of pregnancy so that it does not result in the birth of a child. Abortion can occur naturally. This is known as a miscarriage or spontaneous abortion. An induced or therapeutic abortion is done on purpose to end a pregnancy.

About 90 percent of abortions are performed during the first 12 weeks of pregnancy. Abortion to end an unwanted pregnancy is common. It is estimated that 1 out of every 3 women will have had an abortion during their lives.

Abortion can be done by one of three methods:

Medical abortion can only be performed before 7 weeks of pregnancy. No surgery is necessary. Two drugs are used in a medical abortion, methotrexate and misoprostol. Methotrexate is given in a shot form in the arm or the buttocks, and then 5 to 7 days later the woman inserts 4 misoprostol tablets into her vagina. The uterus then contracts, or moves to become smaller, which causes the pregnancy tissue to come out of the vagina.

Seeking help

It's important to seek help as soon as you think you might be pregnant.

The U.S. Law on Abortion

In the famous 1973 case Roe v. Wade, the Supreme Court ruled that women have a constitutional right to choose an abortion if they would like to terminate their pregnancy. In Roe v. Wade, the Supreme Court ruled that women may choose an abortion up to the point where a fetus is viable, or when it can survive on its own outside the mother's uterus.

In the 1992 case Planned Parenthood v. Casey, the Supreme Court said that government could pass laws about abortion as long as the laws did not attempt to "place a substantial obstacle in the path of a woman seeking an abortion." As a result, recent legislation has been enacted which has changed the original Roe v. Wade ruling. The changes are as follows:

A 14 states now require a mandatory waiting period of up to 24 hours before a woman is able to receive an abortion.

B 29 states currently require parental involvement (parent consent or notification) in order for a minor (under 18 years old) to receive an abortion.

C In states where parental consent laws are in place, a teen can obtain an abortion without a parent's consent through a process called judicial bypass. The teen must go before a judge and explain why the parent did not agree to the abortion, or prove that she can make the decision on her own.

Suction termination of pregnancy, or Suction Curettage is by far the most common form of abortion. It is a surgical procedure and can be done through the fourteenth week of pregnancy. It is an operation done under local or general anesthetic and lasts between 5 and 15 minutes. A suction tube gently sucks the lining and tissue in the uterus. Most women recover quickly and go home the same day.

Rights and wrongs
Many people have strong feelings about the ethics of abortion. These women are demonstrating for and against a law about abortion.

Mifepristone, also known as RU-486 or the "early abortion pill," is another drug that can cause an abortion. It is taken along with another drug called misoprostol. Used in Europe since 1988, this method was just declared safe and legal for use in the United States in September, 2000. It can be used when a woman is up to seven weeks pregnant.

Is it killing?
Many people argue that abortion is an illegal killing.

Answers to Ann's questions

Ann thinks that abortion might be the best choice for her and Nick, but she has a lot of questions:

- Will she be able to become pregnant in the future? If the abortion goes smoothly, there is no risk to her future ability to conceive.

- Will it hurt? The operation is not painful, but is often followed by period-like pain and bleeding for a few days.

- Will anyone else know about the operation? Depending on the state she lives in, Ann may require permission from her parent or guardian. If Ann lives in a state where parent permission is not required, she will receive totally confidential care.

- Will the fetus feel pain? There is no scientific evidence that the fetus at less than 26 weeks is able to feel.

Finding out that you are pregnant can be scary and confusing. Often teens don't know who to turn to or what services are available to them. They react in different ways.

Some young women enter a phase of denial about being pregnant. They have heard that periods can stop if you feel under pressure or have lost a lot of weight. The idea of talking to a professional person or to their parents about the possibility of being pregnant is much too difficult. They deny their pregnancy and continue without any prenatal care and eventually go into labor and give birth with no preparation.

Other women deliberately hide their pregnancy. They make a decision to move away from their home and community and proceed with the pregnancy in privacy. Sometimes they are very organized, seek professional help, have prenatal care, deliver the baby safely, and then give it up for adoption. They can then return home as though nothing had happened. They do, however, remain weighed down by the burden of their secrecy.

Often, having concealed their pregnancy, women are still afraid to seek professional help. They give birth to their babies out of the hospital and with no assistance. In this case the young woman is totally unprepared for motherhood and looking after a new baby. The desperation of the situation can lead her to extremes of behavior. Sometimes these women feel so desperate and afraid that they may abandon their babies. Often the baby is left in a public place and is found by a person in the community.

Paperboy finds baby under bush

A PAPERBOY found a newborn baby abandoned under a bush in freezing weather as he bicycled home from his paper route.

Mother of abandoned baby says "I want her to have a special life"

Babies find haven in mailbox

A BAPTIST minister has built a steel "delivery box" into a wall of her Johannesburg church to tackle a growing crisis of abandoned babies in South Africa. Unwanted infants can now be "mailed" there by their mothers rather than being left to die in places such as gàrbage cans or dump. In the first three months, 13 babies have been delivered through this "Door of Hope."

Germans "mail" unwanted babies

A BABY-BANK where mothers can safely abandon unwanted infants by pushing them through a hatch into the care of social workers is to open in Germany.

It is important to get help as soon as you think you might be pregnant. You do not have to go through it alone! The sooner you talk to someone, the sooner you can get help and decide what you would like to do about the pregnancy. Talk to a trusted adult, such as a parent, counselor, teacher, doctor, nurse, or adult family friend. It is normal to have a wide number of feelings about being pregnant. You may feel happy and excited, yet sad and scared at the same time. This is normal, but it is important to explore your feelings with a trusted adult.

Infanticide

Pregnant teens often worry about how having a baby will change their lives. Many worry about having enough money to care for the baby, how they will achieve their education and future goals, as well as how they will have to grow up fast.

Many women report feeling depressed after giving birth. They may feel happy one minute, yet sad the next. They may feel happy to have a new baby, but also feel very sad sometimes and as if they cannot cope with the needs of the baby. This is called postpartum depression. About 10 percent of women become seriously depressed after childbirth. Doctors can help these women who experience postpartum depression.

Depression

Mothers with postpartum depression find it hard to enjoy the new baby.

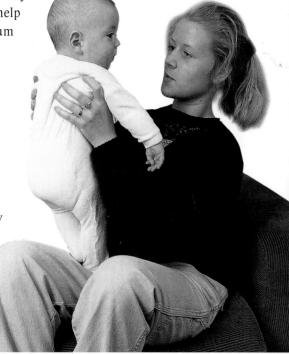

Unwanted pregnancy can be avoided when young people understand their relationships and are thoughtful about whether a relationship has reached a stage where starting to have sexual intercourse is right for them. Young couples need to be able to communicate their feelings and have confidence and trust in each other, and they also need practical knowledge in order to obtain and use adequate contraception.

6 Avoiding Pregnancy
Relationships and Contraception

Shelley talks:
"You hear all the boys
talking about scoring with the girls.
It seems to make them feel cool. But they're
mean about the girls they know have had sex, calling
them cheap and easy. I only want to have sex when
I'm really in love. It matters to me that the
right boy will really care for me. I
think sex is special, so I'll
save it until then."

As we've already previously covered, sexual intercourse can result in the creation of a baby. It's important to think about the consequences of sexual intercourse and the realities of teen pregnancy and parenthood, and how to protect yourself from an unwanted pregnancy. Deciding whether or not the time is right for you to be sexually active can be a difficult decision. It is important to think about how we build relationships in which sex becomes important, as well as how we communicate within these relationships.

Relationships

When, as a teenager, you start to develop emotional and sexual relationships, your feelings have been influenced by all your past experiences of contact with other people—most likely starting with the very dependent relationship with your parent when you were first born. We are all brought up in a huge variety of ways, in different cultures, and with different religions. We may live with two birth parents, one parent, in a step-family, or in an extended family. Our attitudes toward relationships are affected by those we have seen around us—which could mean parents developing an equal and caring relationship, and hugging and kissing in our company; or abusive relationships between the adults close to us; or unequal partnerships where one person physically or emotionally dominates the other.

Also, through childhood and adolescence, we develop the skills to express our feelings within relationships. If we always bottle up our feelings, whether we are sad or happy, it becomes more and more difficult to share them with others. We need to learn to recognize the people with whom it is safe to share our feelings. To do that, we have to learn mutual trust. Some feelings and worries can be shared with our parents. Sometimes it is easier to confide in a trusted friend or a brother or sister. When, as teenagers, we start to develop more intimate relationships with just one person, we use all these "interpersonal" skills that we have been learning.

Tony talks:
"It's difficult with
my friends. All the guys
seem to talk about at school is
whether you've done it with someone yet.
I'm not sure they all have, even though they brag.
But it seems that sex is all that counts. I really like
Tina. She said she loved me once. It felt
really good. I really respect her. But
it's really hard to know how
to tell her that I care
about her."

Puberty—A Time for Many Changes

Puberty is the stage of development when young people develop into adults, both emotionally and physically. As the external changes of puberty occur, the sex organs are also developing and producing the hormones that help to produce sex drive. Puberty is a time of many changes, and many new feelings.

In boys this hormone is testosterone. During puberty many obvious things happen—hair grows under the arms, in the pubic area and on the face, the testicles and penis get bigger, and the voice starts to break. But the presence of testosterone is also starting to stir other feelings. Boys start noticing that when they think of something sexually attractive, they get an erection (the penis becomes bigger, stiff, and upright). It can be embarrassing sometimes, for example, when a boy is watching TV with friends and an erection develops at the sight of a sexy scene. Other things also start happening. Boys may have sexual dreams in which they ejaculate (pump semen from the penis). Waking up after a so-called "wet dream" with sticky, damp bedding can be alarming the first time it happens.

Obvious changes also happen to girls during puberty. Body shape changes, hips become broader, hair grows under the arms and in the pubic area, the breasts develop, and periods start. In girls, the ovaries start producing the female hormones estrogen and progesterone.

Sexual attraction means the desire to be very physically close to another person to whom you are attracted. When you are close, your feelings can be different from those you have experienced before. The feelings come from inside you. You start to feel excited, warm inside, and tingly. Boys may develop an erection. Girls may notice the vagina becoming moist and warm. Dealing with these new feelings can be both exciting and frightening. The feelings

Crushes

First emotional attractions as teenagers can be varied. It is very common to have "crushes." These are a safe way of testing some of the strong emotions and feelings that are developing. You can have crushes on all sorts of people, from pop stars to friends at school, from someone your own age to older people, such as your teachers. They can be on someone of the same sex or someone of the opposite sex.

New feelings
When we feel very close to someone, sexual feelings are aroused.

can be so strong that they drive young people to have sexual intercourse without giving thought to that possibility in advance. When intercourse occurs, pregnancy is always a possible outcome.

Safe sex

Strong feelings and desires often lead young people into sexual relationships. How can you insure that such a relationship does not lead to an unwanted pregnancy or sexually transmitted infections?

There are many ways of having a physically satisfying and happy relationship without sexual intercourse. Kissing, hugging, stroking, massaging, and fondling are all sexy and safe. Exploring each other's bodies in these ways helps you learn what feels safe and nonthreatening, and what feels good and exciting. It allows you to express your feelings to your partner, while at the same time reducing your risk for unwanted pregnancy and sexually transmitted infections (STIs).

It can be difficult to decide if it is the right time for you to be sexually active. Many pressures make the idea of sex very attractive. Magazines and movies make sex look very glamorous and exciting. You can feel pressure to have sex from your friends. You may feel that if you have a girlfriend or boyfriend then you "have to" have sex. If you think that all your friends have started sexual relationships, you may feel unhappy about being left behind. It is important to think about what is right for you, and only you. You have the right to decide when the time is "right" to engage in sexual activity.

Understanding your feelings and being prepared to express your emotions can help you to be prepared and ready to develop a mature and satisfying relationship in which you have sex at the time that you and your partner are both ready for it. This will include having arranged for contraception to avoid unwanted pregnancy.

Contraception

Understanding sexual feelings and emotions prepares you to delay starting sexual relations until you are really ready. But when you do start having sex, how do you avoid pregnancy? Contraception (which literally means stopping conception) is the way couples try to prevent pregnancy despite having sexual intercourse. Different methods of contraception are:

Barrier contraception (putting a physical barrier between sperm and egg):
Male condoms are made of thin latex. They are rolled onto the erect penis just before the penis is inserted into the vagina. At ejaculation, the semen is trapped in the condom, thus preventing pregnancy. Used properly, condoms are 97 percent effective at preventing pregnancy. They are the only form of contraception that also protects against sexually transmitted infections and HIV. They can also be used to prevent transmission of STIs and HIV during oral and anal sex.

Double Protection

Protect yourself even more against pregnancy and sexually transmitted infections by using the pill or another form of contraception plus a condom. This has two advantages. First, it makes contraception and therefore the avoidance of pregnancy even more reliable. Second, it protects against sexually transmitted infections.

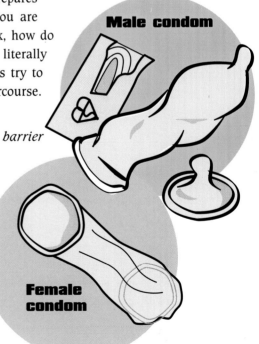

Male condom

Female condom

The **female condom** is made of thin polyurethane plastic. It is placed into the vagina and also covers the area outside the vagina as well. It keeps sperm from entering the vagina. The female condom is 95 percent effective and protects against sexually transmitted infections and HIV. The male condom cannot be used at the same time if you are using the female condom.

The **diaphragm** is a dome-shaped rubber cup which is inserted into the vagina before sex and covers the cervix. It prevents sperm from entering the uterus. It should be used with spermicide, which is a sperm killing chemical, and should be put in up to six hours before sex, and must not be removed until at least six hours after sex. The diaphragm is washed after use and can be reused. The correct size of the diaphragm must be determined after examination by a doctor. It is 94 percent effective. It does not protect against sexually transmitted infections and HIV.

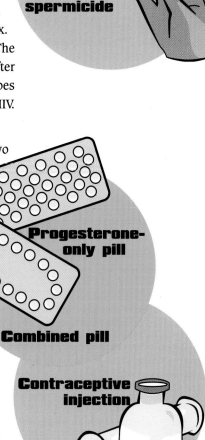

Diaphragm and spermicide

Progesterone-only pill

Combined pill

Contraceptive injection

Hormonal methods of contraception (used by women):
The **combined pill** is made from a combination of the two female hormones, estrogen and progesterone. It works by preventing the release of an egg from the ovary. The combined pill is prescribed by a doctor. It does not protect against sexually transmitted infections and HIV. Taking the pill can have other advantages such as reducing the effects of premenstrual syndrome (PMS), reducing period pain, and making periods lighter and more regular. There are many types of this pill to suit different women's needs. It is 99 percent effective.

The **progesterone-only pill** works by making the mucus of the cervix a more efficient barrier to sperm and by thinning the lining of the uterus to prevent implantation of a fertilized egg. It is useful for some women who are unable to take the combined pill for medical reasons and is 98 percent effective. It must be prescribed by a doctor. It does not protect against sexually transmitted infections and HIV.

A **contraceptive injection** (shot), also commonly known as Depo-Provera, is an injection of progesterone that releases a small amount of progesterone regularly into the body, therefore stopping ovulation. Injections are received in the arm or buttocks, and one shot protects against pregnancy for three months. It is 99 percent effective, but does not protect against sexually transmitted infections and HIV.

Intrauterine methods:

An **IUD** (intrauterine device) is a T-shaped plastic device with a coil of copper around the stem. It is inserted through the cervix and into the uterus by a doctor. It works by stopping sperm meeting the egg and/or by stopping the fertilized egg from implanting in the uterus. The IUD is not suitable for everyone. It is not usually advised for women who have never had a baby. It may make periods heavier and more painful. It is 98 percent effective. It does not protect against sexually transmitted infections or HIV.

Natural methods

To practice this method of contraception, the woman must learn to recognize the stage of her menstrual cycle at which she ovulates. She then avoids intercourse at this time, because it is an "unsafe period" and pregnancy is likely to occur during this very fertile period. There are also devices that women who have a regular cycle can use to try to detect the timing of ovulation. Natural methods are not recommended for teenagers because their menstrual cycles are often irregular and it can be very difficult to predict ovulation because of this. There is also no protection against sexually transmitted infections and it is quite possible that the days a woman is fertile can change from month to month. This method is also only 94 percent effective.

Emergency contraception

This is contraception that is used after unprotected sex. Unprotected sex is sex where no contraception

The emergency pill

The emergency contraceptive pill is often called the "morning after pill." Emergency contraception can be used within 72 hours (3 days) after unprotected intercourse. However, the earlier it is used, the more effective it is.

has been used, or if contraception was used the method failed—for example, a birth control pill was missed, or the condom has burst. There are two types of emergency hormonal contraception. The combined form is a high strength of the combined pill, taken in two doses 12 hours apart. It may work by stopping ovulation or by preventing implantation of the fertilized egg. It is 50 percent effective if used after sex at the most fertile time of the menstrual cycle. The new form of emergency hormonal contraception is a progesterone-only form, again taken in two doses 12 hours apart. It works in a similar way but is more effective and has fewer side effects. It is nearly 75 percent effective.

An emergency IUD can be inserted up to five days after unprotected intercourse and then used as a long-term method of contraception. It is 98 percent effective.

Cultural and Religious Factors in Contraception

Some people may not find it morally possible to use all types of contraception. Different religions give different guidance about what contraception, if any, is acceptable. For example, the Catholic Church does not accept any artificial forms of contraception. The only methods that practicing Catholics may use are natural methods or abstinence.

Termination of pregnancy is also not permissible. Islamic rule allows the majority of forms of contraception to be used only by married couples in order to space the children in a family. Other world religions, such as Hinduism, Judaism, and Buddhism, also have rules about the types of contraception that are acceptable. You may want to think about your own cultural or religious beliefs when choosing the right contraceptive method for you. It is important that you feel comfortable and secure with the method you choose, and that it fits in with your beliefs.

The Catholic view
Catholic guidance about contraception and abortion is very strict. The pope, the head of the Catholic Church, explains the Church's beliefs and teachings.

7 The Future
Increasing
Choices

Life will not stand still. Facilities for planning and managing your fertility will progress beyond what is available now.

IVF

A view through the microscope of a human egg being injected with sperm. On the left is a pipette used to hold the egg in place while the injection is carried out.

Contraception

In the field of contraception, research is constantly moving forward. Scientists are working to make the best contraceptives that are safe, reliable, easy to use, and hazard-free. Efforts are being made to make a barrier contraception method that is effective and more pleasant to use than condoms and that can be combined with chemical gels that may kill both sperm and sexually transmitted viruses.

Hormonal contraception for women will continue to improve. New ways of giving it will be found, such as by patch: a sticky patch is attached to the skin and the hormone is absorbed through the skin. Maybe other chemicals will become available that need to be taken only once a month. The "male pill" might be developed, finding a hormonal way to block sperm production.

The IUD is being improved, making it much smaller—effectively a single thread that can be attached to the inside of the uterus. This will make the IUD easier to use for women who have never had children.

In the future, maybe methods will be developed that stop the production of sperm or the release of eggs until the man or woman wishes to be fertile. Other techniques, such as using chemicals that prevent the implantation of the fertilized egg in the uterus or possibly immunizing women against sperm, are in the early stages of investigation.

Fertility Management

Fertility management is the use of science and technology to assist humans in reproducing. Fertility management is currently used to help individuals who are having difficulty becoming pregnant. Artificial means of solving the problem are becoming more and more successful. The most common method used is in vitro fertilization (IVF), also sometimes referred to as the development of a "test-tube baby." The process involves removing eggs from a woman's ovary and fertilizing the egg with the male's sperm in the laboratory. The fertilized egg is then implanted into the woman's uterus.

The world's first successful IVF baby was Louise Brown, born in England in 1978. Her birth gave hope to many infertile couples. Since then IVF has continued to advance. The success of the basic procedure opened the way to many possibilities for the future, moving the frontiers both scientifically and ethically.

Scientists are also experimenting with controlling the genes in embryos. This is called genetic manipulation. Genes are the parts of cells that determine what characteristics a baby inherits from his or her parents. Genetic manipulation will be used to help with the management of inherited diseases. It may also be used to allow parents to choose what sex the baby will be, what eye color the baby will have, and so on. As a result, the science fiction concept of a "designer baby" may become a reality.

The baby who launched a revolution

LOUISE BROWN, the world's first test-tube child, is 21 ...

Doctor offers choice of baby's sex

A **DOCTOR** specializing in in vitro fertilization is to launch the world's first fertility service to create babies of whichever sex their parents require.

Gay men expecting twins

TWO wealthy gay men caused an angry response from family groups yesterday after bypassing British law to allow them to become the parents of surrogate twins, due to be born in the United States.

OLDER WOMEN AND IVF

A 63-year-old woman who lied about her age to get IVF treatment has become the oldest woman to give birth to a healthy baby. Her case has led to renewed questions of ethics and whether there should be an age limit on becoming a parent.

As women get older, there is an increased chance of having a baby affected by chromosomal abnormalities such as Down's syndrome. To avoid this, in the future, it may become possible for women to store ovarian tissue while they are young to use at a later date.

Further advances in fertility management, and perhaps also in the production of therapies for medical problems, may be possible by using the technique of cloning. Cloning is the use of science and technology to create an exact copy of an organism's genetic material. Cloning was used to produce Dolly the sheep. The cloning technique, also known as "cell nuclear transfer," involves taking an egg and removing its nucleus (the part of the cell containing genetic material). The nucleus is then replaced with the nucleus from an adult cell. Before the transfer, the genetic material in the replacement nucleus could be manipulated to make new characteristics in the baby.

At the present time, cloning of humans has not occurred. Research is progressing fast in animals, with one of the goals being to produce animals that will be able to donate organs to humans, such as kidneys for kidney

Dolly
Cloning produced Dolly the sheep in 1997.

transplantations. It may be possible to produce animals that will make blood products that can be used in humans.

There has been much debate about cloning, particularly about the possibility of cloning humans in the future. Some people believe it is "wrong," while some people believe it is "right." Many people argue in favor of human cloning, and believe it should be used to help infertile couples, to help lesbian women to have children, or to produce an exact genetic copy of a child lost by stillbirth, illness, or accident. Further debate and discussion will be needed to sort out how appropriate these ideas are for human life.

And the Rest of the World

While the Western world is struggling with the issues that arise from what scientists are offering in the fields of biology and genetics, much of the rest of the world still lives in extreme poverty. World population growth is greater than the growth of world food production.

A midwife
A UNICEF midwife visits a pregnant mother in a village in Malawi.

In 1994, an international conference held in Cairo investigated the problems of world population growth. From the origins of man until 1800 A.D., the world's human population grew to reach 1 billion. The next 5 billion people were added in 200 years. It has taken only 12 years for the last 1 billion people to be added. The size of the world's population has increased more in the last 50 years than in the previous million years!

The largest increase in population occurs in countries with the greatest poverty and unemployment. Ninety-seven percent of the future world population growth will be in developing countries, with the highest growth rate in Africa.

Governments around the world have responded in different ways to the problem of the rapidly increasing sizes of their populations. In the 1960s, the average family size in developing countries was six children. But advances in public health, such as the availability of vaccinations (shots) against common diseases, made children much healthier and far fewer family members were dying in childhood. It became important to find ways of slowing the growth of the population.

China developed its "one child policy" in 1979. Families were given incentives, or rewards, to persuade them to have only one child. Families who had only one child were given financial rewards and access to better housing and schools. This policy was quickly successful in lowering population growth: the number of births per woman fell on average from 6 children to 2 children over a period of only 20 years.

Other countries, such as Bangladesh and some in Africa, have achieved success in other ways. They have rapidly expanded access to contraception. They no longer need

Two approaches
China's "one child policy" assisted in lowering the country's birthrate, but other approaches may be just as successful. In Gambia, health workers go out into the community and explain contraception.

medical staff to prescribe contraception, but sell it over the counter, or use trained field workers to take contraception to people in rural villages. These techniques, used along with improved education and expectations, particularly for young women, have helped to reduce the birth rate.

On average, in the developing world, the number of births per woman has fallen during the last 30 years from 6 children to 3 children. But there are still huge variations around the world. Health risks are much higher in developing countries. In those countries 2 million children die every year of diseases that could be prevented by vaccination. 7.5 million newborn babies die every year because their mothers have received poor health care during pregnancy and childbirth.

Two hundred million children do not have proper nutrition. Two hundred million poor people in the world do not have access to contraception. Deaths of women related to pregnancy and childbirth are 250 times more common than in developed countries.

In the developed world, we are fortunate. If we choose, we can obtain contraception. We can choose our relationships and plan to have our children at stages in our lives that are better for us. We can be much more confident that, when we have children, they will be healthy and live until an old age. We have a duty to future generations to use all these advantages wisely.

Teenagers and the Future

There are more teenagers in the world today than ever before. Answers to questions about the future lie in their hands.

Resources

The following organizations provide information for young people about sexuality and pregnancy:

Planned Parenthood Federation of America
1-800-230-PLAN
This national number can refer you to the nearest Planned Parenthood clinic. Planned Parenthood provides family planning, abortion, and women's health services, as well as information about sexuality issues. Website: www.plannedparenthood.org

Sexuality Information and Education Council of the United States (SEICUS)
130 West 42nd Street, Suite 350
New York, NY 10036
(212) 819-9770
Website: www.siecus.org
Provides a wide variety of information on sexuality education and issues; has an on-site library that is open to the public.

National Abortion Federation
1-800-424-2280 (toll free)
Provides information on abortion and parental consent laws for teenagers, as well as referrals to family planning clinics and abortion services.

Emergency Contraception Hotline
1-800-584-9911 (toll free)
Information on Emergency Contraception Pills (ECPs), also called the "morning after pill," as well as referrals to the nearest health clinic that provides ECPs.

Centers for Disease Control National STD and HIV/AIDS Hotline
1-800-342-AIDS (toll free in English)
1-800-344-SIDA (toll free in Spanish)
1-800-243-7889 (TTY) (toll free, Deaf Access)

Answers questions about STDs, HIV and AIDS, and provides referrals for counseling and testing.

New York Civil Liberties Union Reproductive Rights Project Teen Health Initiative
125 Broad Street, 17th Floor
New York, NY 10004
(212) 344-3005
Website: www.nyclu.org
Provides legal information on the health care rights of teenagers living in New York State. Publishes a number of pamphlets which explain the health rights of teens and the rights of pregnant/parenting teenagers.

Covenant House/The Nine Line
1-800-999-9999
A 24 hour hotline for teens in crisis.

Department of Health Clinics
In every county, there is a Department of Health which provides teens with medical care, information, and referrals for contraceptives, as well as testing for STIs and HIV. Look for the phone number of your county's Department of Health in your phone book.

WORLD WIDE WEB RESOURCES:

www.gynpages.com/acol
Provides a complete list of abortion providers in every state.

www.goaskalice.columbia.edu
Sponsored by the Columbia University Health Services, this website answers questions from readers about sex, contraception, relationships, and other issues.

www.teenwire.com
Sponsored by Planned Parenthood Federation of the United States, this teen-specific website focuses on a variety of issues.

RECOMMENDED READING:

Bell, Ruth. *Changing Bodies, Changing Lives*. New York: Random House, 1998. Filled with quotes from teens, this book provides information on a number of topics, including sexuality, STIs, contraception, school issues, and family relationships.

Gray, Heather M., and Samantha Phillips. *Real Girl Real World: Tools for Finding Your True Self*. Seattle, WA: Seal Press, 1995. This book presents a straightforward discussion of sexuality and related issues for teenage girls.

Harris, Robie H. *It's Perfectly Normal: Changing Bodies, Sex, and Sexual Health*, New York: Penguin, 1994.

Isler, R.N., Charlotte, and Alywn T. Cohall, M.D. *The Watts Teen Health Dictionary*. Danbury, CT: Franklin Watts, 1996. Your questions about sexuality and other health issues are answered in this dictionary-style book.

Kuklin, S. *What Do I Do Now? Talking About Teenage Pregnancy*. New York: G.P. Putnam's Sons, 1991.

Lindsay, Jeanne Warren. *Teens Parenting*, Buena Park, CA: Morning Glory Press, 1991.

Sex and the law in the US

There are no laws in any state that require parental consent if a teen who is under 18 years old wants to get birth control or other forms of contraception.

The legal age of consent for sexual intercourse varies from state to state, but in most states, a teen is thought to be able to consent to sex if they are 16 to 17 years old.

It is illegal for an adult (someone who is over 18 years of age) to have sexual intercourse with a minor (someone under 18 years old). This is called statutory rape and it is a crime that is punishable by law.

Twenty-nine states currently require parental consent and/or parental notification in order for a teen who is a minor (under 18 years of age) to receive an abortion.

Glossary

prenatal care   medical care given to a woman during pregnancy to care for the woman and developing baby; helps the baby to be born healthy.

conception   the joining of sperm and egg to start a pregnancy.

congenital abnormality   an abnormality caused by damage to the developing fetus in the uterus.

contraception   methods used to avoid conception or, in other words, to avoid pregnancy despite having sexual intercourse.

embryo   the very early cellular stage of development of a baby in the uterus.

fertility   a person's ability to conceive.

fetus   the developing unborn baby; the baby is called a fetus beginning in the third month of pregnancy.

hormone   chemical messenger produced in a gland in the body.

labor   the process of the contraction of the uterus to push the baby down through the vagina, to give birth.

midwife   nurse who looks after women during pregnancy and delivery and immediately after birth.

obstetrician   doctor who specializes in caring for women during pregnancy and delivery.

ovary   female gonad or site of production of eggs and the female hormones estrogen and progesterone.

ovulation   the release of an egg from the ovary.

ovum   the egg from a female; it is released from the female's ovary once a month.

postnatal care   medical and nursing care given to mothers and babies after delivery.

postpartum depression   depression that often occurs in the months after giving birth to a baby.

pregnancy test   method of detecting whether or not a woman is pregnant by looking at the hormone levels that are present in either her urine or blood.

"safe sex"   having oral, anal, or penile-vaginal (penis to vagina) sex using methods of contraception to lessen the risk of pregnancy and sexually transmitted infections.

sexually transmitted infections (STIs)   infections that are transmitted during oral, anal, or penile-vaginal (penis to vagina) sexual activity.

sperm   produced in the testes, this male reproductive cell is microscopic and shaped like a tadpole; if a sperm cell fertilizes an egg, a baby can develop.

spontaneous abortion   medical term for miscarriage, when the pregnancy is lost naturally.

testes   male gonad or site of production of sperm and the male hormone testosterone.

therapeutic abortion   medically known as a termination of pregnancy; the ending of a pregnancy so that it does not result in the birth of a baby.

ultrasound scan   test using sound waves to take a picture of the baby in the uterus.

Index